DIVINE
MILESTONES

To: Undraxh Ungut-od

DIVINE MILESTONES

A Global Vision
Beyond The American Dream

2/4/2020

David Sohn

Library of Congress Control Number: 2016905933
ISBN: Hardcover   978-1-5144-8417-3
              Softcover   978-1-5144-8416-6
              eBook   978-1-5144-8415-9

Print information available on the last page.

Rev. date: 04/13/2016

To order additional copies of this book, contact:
Xlibris
1-888-795-4274
www.Xlibris.com
Orders@Xlibris.com
740159

Contents

DIVINE MILESTONES

A Global Vision Beyond The American Dream

David Sohn, D.M.

CHAPTER 1

TRAVEL PLAN

1.1 Google Maps Driving Directions

I always thank God for allowing us to invent state-of-the-art technologies for our daily lives, among many of His graces and gifts given to human beings. Nowadays, many drivers use automobile navigators to plan for their trips by finding out the distance and time to the destination, alternative routes, and milestones.

For example, a tourist who completed touring the Empire State Building located at 350 Fifth Avenue, New York, NY 10118 is wants to plan to visit the White House located at 1600 NW Pennsylvania Avenue, Washington, D.C. 20500.

The tourist decides to rent a car and drive to the White House, although alternatively he can take a train from New York's Penn Station to Union Station in Washington, D.C. Another option is a flight from JFK to Ronald Reagan National Airport.

He uses Google Maps for driving directions from the Empire State Building to the White House. Google Maps shows that the distance is approximately 231 miles, and it would take more than four hours as shown in the Google Map below.

DRIVING DIRECTIONS

FROM: **Empire State Building**
350 5th Ave., New York

TO: **The White House**
1600 Pennsylvania Ave., NW, Washington, DC

(About 4 hours/230 miles)

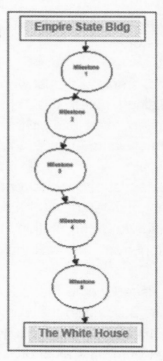

Start Point: Leave Empire State Building

Milestone 1: Get on NY-495 W Highway

Milestone 2: Take I-95 S -> NJ Turnpike S -> I-95 S ->I895 S

Milestone 3: Baltimore-Washington PKWY

Milestone 4: Maine Ave SW

Milestone 5: 15th St NW

Destination: Arrive at The White House

The above driving directions show five major milestones from departure to destination:

Departure: Empire State Building

Milestone 1: Get on NY-495 W (10 minutes; 11 miles)

Milestone 2: Take I-95 S -> NJ Turnpike S -> I-95 S ->I895 S

Milestone 3: Baltimore-Washington PKWY

Milestone 4: Maine Ave SW

Milestone 5: 15th St NW

Arrive: **The White House**

1.3 Importance of Travel Plan and Milestones

We often take business and personal trips out of state or out of the country. The farther we travel, the more detailed plan we tend to make. When we plan to drive a longer distance, we have to make a detailed and thorough travel plan to save time and money. Detailed plans include a number of important factors, such as day and time of travel and weather. For example, the tourist who wants to drive from the Empire State Building to the White House will have to choose his departure time to avoid rush hours in some parts of his journey.

However, whichever travel plan we make, it is imperative for us to set definite milestones to reach our destination faster and easily. For example, the tourist must take Milestone 2: Take I-95 S. Otherwise, he will not be able to reach the destination within four hours.

In summary, we must make thorough travel plans and set important milestones to achieve the entire travel plans most successfully. This principle of setting milestones to achieve a plan successfully is applicable to any type of plan we make, whether the plan is for a simple task, project, or lifetime vision.

CHAPTER 2

GOD'S PLAN AND MILESTONES FOR THE UNIVERSE

2.1 God's Plan for the Universe

Although I knew God created the universe, including all human beings, I never thought about God's plan for the universe. Although there are a number of scholars and theologians who define God's plan for the universe, David Sulem describes God's milestones for Him to achieve His plan for the universe well in his *God's Plan for All* (November 7, 2014).

David Sulem stated God made a plan to create and deliver the Eternal Kingdom for the Grand Family of God. The Grand Family of God is comprised of God the Father who plans to dwell with all men as the head of the grand family, His Son Jesus Christ, His only begotten Son, all the human beings created and adopted as His children, and all His angels created as His children.

The ultimate purpose of God's plan is for everyone to enter the Eternal Kingdom for the Grand Family of God where there will be no more death, no more pain, no more sorrow, and no more curses, and the Father God will be all in all (1 Corinthians 15:24, 28; Colossians 1:15-20; Revelation 21:1-6).

2.2 God's Milestones to Achieve His Plan for the Universe

God set seven milestones to create and deliver the Eternal Kingdom for the Grand Family of God. According to David Sulem, God divided His plan into seven ages, which are the milestones for God to achieve His plan, as listed below.

Milestone 1: The Pre-Adamic Age

Milestone 2: The Adamic Age

Milestone 3: The Age of Israel under the Old Mosaic Covenant of the Law

Milestone 4: The Age of the Church under the New Covenant of Grace

Milestone 5: The Millennial Age of the Kingdom of God

Milestone 6: The Lake of Fire Judgment Age

Milestone 7: The Eternal Age of the Kingdom of God

CHAPTER 3

GOD'S PLAN FOR ALL HUMAN BEINGS

3.1 God's Plan for All

In accordance with the Bible, God knows "the plans He has for [us], plans to prosper [us] and not to harm [us], plans to give [us] hope and a future" (Jeremiah 29:11, NIV). God also promised He will meet all our needs to His glorious riches in Christ Jesus (Philippians 4:19, NIV).

3.2 God's Determination of Our Steps

According to the Bible, in our heart we plan our course, but "the Lord determines our steps" (Proverbs 16:9, NIV). In reality, however, it may not be God who determines *each and every step* we take. In other words, we take our own steps in our lives. It was not until 1968 when I realized God had plans for me, but He does not necessarily determine each and every step, He directs me to reach out safely and successfully to the next milestone He preset (Proverbs 16:9). This was when I became to know the importance of finding out about God's milestones preset for me to achieve His plan for me.

3.3 God's Free Will Be Given to Us as His Grace

God creates us and leads our life until we die. However, God gives each of us a free will for us to achieve His plan for us. For example, God does not compel us to believe in Jesus Christ for us to have eternal life (John 3:16). In other words, He gives us a free will, although He could create us as "robotic" humans who automatically believe in Jesus Christ from our birth.

God is most pleased when we voluntarily choose to believe in Jesus Christ. In other words, He has given us the free gift of salvation if we choose to believe in Jesus.

There are many verses where God pleads to our free will.

Jesus Christ says, "Here I am! I stand at the door and knock. If anyone hears my voice and opens the door, I will come in and eat with that person, and they with me" (Revelation 3:20, NIV). Jesus could come into our room even without knocking the door and asking us to eat. However, He asks us to open the door only when we wish.

God creates us in His own image (Genesis 1:27) as human beings, but not as His children from our birth. He predestines us to be adopted as His children only through Jesus Christ, in accordance with His pleasure and will (Ephesians 1:5). In other words, He gives us a free will to become His children.

In summary, God presets milestones in our lifetime to achieve His plan for us but He allows us to exercise our free will to take routes different from His "preferred" optimal route. Regardless of the route we choose to take, God leads us to the next milestone.

CHAPTER 4

GOD'S PLAN FOR ME

God created me in His image (Genesis 1:27) in 1939 in a small rural farm in Korea. I never asked myself or anyone else about why He created me, until 1968 when I was thirty years old.

On January 5, 1968, I started a brand new civilian job as a news reporter after I was medically discharged from the Korean Army as of December 31, 1967. My salary was one-fifth of that in the Korean Army.

My daily assignments were to search out and dig out all the corruptive, unfair, unjust, and irrational matters deeply rooted for long inside the public and private sectors and write those in news articles. The more realistic and cruel articles I wrote, the more financial awards were given to me by my employer. The more I tried to dig out corruption, the more people tried to "buy" me.

I worked for four months, but I could not tolerate the corruptive phenomena deeply rooted in the society any longer. This was the turning point in my life, and I resigned from my employer on April 30, 1968. This was also when I asked myself why God created me. Then I was convinced God created me with a special purpose unknown to me. I also thought His plan for me might be uniquely different from His plans given to other people.

I tried hard to find out what God's plan for me was. I had to remember all the steps I took from birth to April 30, 1968, when I resigned from the news reporter job.

This was the time I believed God's plan was for me to transform the Korean society and the world through innovative and effective education. This was when I realized God led me to find a job as a news reporter and witness all the corruptions and irrational realities. Otherwise, I would never have thought about God's plan for me.

On May 1, 1968, I set my lifetime vision to, "transform the Korean society and ultimately the entire world through innovative and effective education." I believe God's plan for me was exactly the same as the lifetime vision I set for myself based on my prayer, faith, and the milestones I have achieved (Proverbs 16:9).

CHAPTER 5

PAST SEVEN MILESTONES SET BY ME

5.1 God's Conception of Milestones Preset for Me

On May 1, 1968, I concluded God's plan for me was I transform the Korean society and the world. Although God determines my steps (Proverbs 16:9), I realized I, not God, chose *all* the steps I took until I was thirty years old. First, I was suspicious of Proverbs 16:9, which says, "A man's heart plans his way, but the Lord directs his steps." However, immediately I interpreted the verse contextually, not literally. In other words, the term "his steps" does not mean *each and every step* the man takes, but a general way or direction he should take. In other words, God does not direct each and every step we should take, but He directs and guides us in the right direction until we arrive at the next *milestone* safely and successfully.

5.2 Free Will Given to Me as a God's Grace According to His Pleasure

I also realized God does not direct each and every step of mine from one milestone to the next milestone because He is most pleased when I arrive at the next milestone successfully as a result of my own free will, not His direction.

There are many passages where God gives us a free will. For example, God creates us in His image, and we become a creature (Genesis 1:27). He wants all of us to become His children not by His "force," but by our free will. In Ephesians 1:5 (NIV), "He predestined us for adoption to sonship through Jesus Christ, in accordance with his pleasure and will." He could create us as **robots** that can do whatever He wants us to do, but He does not create us as robots.

John 3:16 (NIV) says, "God so loved the world that He gave His one and only Son, that whoever believes in Him shall not perish but have eternal life." He could give us eternal life when He creates us, but He does not. He wants us to find out who Jesus Christ is and choose Him as our Lord and Savior at our own will, not by His force.

In Revelation 3:20 (NIV), Jesus said, "Here I am! I stand at the door and knock. If anyone hears my voice and opens the door, I will come in and eat with that person, and they with me." He could kick the door, come in the room and say, "Let's eat," however, He does not. He wants to eat with us only when and if we recognize Him as Jesus and open the door.

5.3 Past Seven Milestones Set By Me According to God's Plan

I became to know God's plan for me in 1968 when I was thirty years old. However, I believed He set certain milestones for me to live a successful life for the past thirty years from my birth. I tried hard to find out about the past milestones, and there were seven milestones from my birth to 1968, when I was thirty years old, as follows:

Milestone 1:   God created me in His image (Genesis 1:27).

Milestone 2:   God led me to achieve academic superiority.

Milestone 3:   God led me to choose Korea Military Academy.

Milestone 4:   God led me to study at the U.S. Army Signal School.

Milestone 5:   God led me to witness those who achieved the American Dream.

Milestone 6:   God led me to marry Mokjah Kim to adopt us as His son and daughter.

Milestone 7:   God led me to dream of the American Dream.

5.4 Milestone 1: God Created Me in His Image (Genesis 1:27)

I was born in Dangjin, a small rural town in Korea, in 1939. The picture below is the first picture taken with my mother, when I was nine years old. According to the terms used in this century, she was a "Tiger Mom" and "Super Mom." I owe my mother what I am today and everything I have earned. Her entire life was devoted and dedicated to my education.

In summary, God led me to achieve this milestone preset in accordance with God's plan for me (Proverbs 16:9).

5.5 Milestone 2: God Led Me to Achieve Academic Superiority

Koreans start learning the Korean language, which is a phonetic language when they are at a pre-kindergarten age. However, Koreans learn Chinese characters from their elementary schools. Because Chinese characters are difficult to learn, it has been part of the Korean culture that the more Chinese characters Koreans know, the more intelligent and more educated they are recognized and treated as throughout the Korean society for many generations.

This was the reason why my mother forced me to memorize by heart and master one thousand Chinese characters, called *"Chunjamoon,"* in Korean when I was six years old. My mother was so strict that she spanked me cruelly when I failed to memorize some of the assigned characters each day.

I cried and complained a lot, but when I was admitted to the elementary school, I was the only person who knew so many Chinese characters. I was proud and excited to teach Chinese characters not only to my peers but also to our teachers. As a result, I used to be called *"Hanmoon Baksa,"* which means a "doctor of Chinese characters," during my elementary school years.

My mother who was a "Tiger Mom" helped me to have confidence in academic competitions not only during my elementary school days but also during my middle school days and beyond. I attended Dangjin Middle School, which was the largest middle school in the entire borough of Dangjin. I achieved the highest grades in all subjects throughout the 1955 class at Dangjin Middle School. I was proud that I was the recipient of the Grand

Scholarship awarded to the student who achieved the highest academic grades in school.

I went to Incheon High School in Incheon, which is west of Seoul, Korea. After graduation, I was admitted to Yonsei University, which was one of the top three universities in Korea, without taking the entrance examination. However, I went to Korea Military Academy with a full scholarship for tuition, room and board.

5.6 Milestone 3: God Led Me to Choose Korea Military Academy

Although I was admitted to Yonsei University, I could not afford to pay tuition. However, God led me to choose His destined journey. I found out that Korea Military Academy (KMA) offers a Bachelor of Science degree with a full scholarship for tuition, room, and board. After four years of study, cadets were commissioned as a second lieutenant. I also heard about KMA's tough military training that made me hesitate to enter KMA.

While I was indecisive, one of the KMA recruiting officers told me that once I graduated from KMA, there would be many opportunities to work as a military attaché working for Korea's ambassadors to foreign countries. The KMA recruiting officer reminded me of the great leaders of the world graduated from some type of military academy or college. For example, U.S. President Dwight Eisenhower graduated from West Point; British Premier Winston Churchill graduated from the Royal Military College of Sandhurst; and French President Charles De Gaulle graduated from the French Military Academy of Saint-Cyr.

Another reason why I decided to enter KMA was because I scored the highest grade in English during the entrance examination, and the English department chair encouraged me to enroll at KMA.

The military training provided at KMA was similar to what is provided at West Point. In certain areas, KMA training was tougher. The training taken during the first six months was called "Beast Training," during which the cadets were treated as beasts. I almost failed in Beast Training, but I survived.

During my four-years at KMA, I cried a lot and tried to quit, not only because I could not endure all the hardships, but because I was not able to eat meals well. The only hope that kept me until graduation was if I was commissioned as a signal corps officer, then I could go to the U.S. Army Signal School with a full scholarship provided by the U.S. Army.

In summary, God led me to achieve this milestone set in accordance with God's plan for me (Proverbs 16:9).

5.7 Milestone 4: God Led Me to Study at the U.S. Army Signal School

I was forced to withdraw from Yonsei University and chose KMA for my studies, mainly for financial reasons. Although it was my own decision, I found out that God led me to take necessary steps for me to achieve His plan for me: **"To transform the world through the most innovative and effective education provided to all the human beings around the world."**

After I had been commissioned in 1963, I was dispatched to serve as a signal platoon leader along the Demilitarized Zone (DMZ) confronting with the North Korean soldiers. Later I was appointed to an aide-de-camp to assist a general in charge of operations (G3) at the First ROK Army stationed in Wonju, Korea. Among many responsibilities as the aide-de-camp, I had to act as an interpreter between the U.S. Army Colonel of U.S. Advisory Group and the First ROK Army General and translate many official letters into English and Korean between the U.S. Advisory Group and First ROK Army.

I was excited about the job as the aide-de-camp, not only because I was able to practice my English directly with Americans, but also because I learned about the opportunity for me as a signal corps officer to be able to study at the U.S. Army Signal School at Fort Monmouth, New Jersey. Following the Korean War, the Korea Army used the same communications equipment, such as portable radios and telephones, as the U.S. Army. Therefore, ROK Army selects the best-qualified signal corps officers to study at the U.S. Army Signal School through a set of tough and strict competition.

I was one of the officers who passed both English and technical exams sponsored by the ROK Army. Then, I left the aide-de-camp position and entered the ROK Army English School in Youngchon to prepare for the English proficiency test similar to TOEFL. I studied hard for one year to practice English because I felt I had started my journey to fulfill my dream. As a result, I topped the English class and received the ROK Army Chief of Staff Award.

A week after I graduated, I took the TOEFL-like English proficiency test sponsored by the U.S. Advisory Group. Fortunately, I scored highest in the exam, so I was allowed to take the longest course, namely one year, to study at the U.S. Army Signal School at Fort Monmouth, New Jersey from 1966 to 1967.

In summary, God led me to achieve this milestone set in accordance with God's plan for me (Proverbs 16:9).

5.8 Milestone 5: God Led Me to Witness Those Who Achieved the American Dream

I was awarded a full scholarship from the U.S. Army Signal School in Fort Monmouth to study communications and computers from May 1966 for one year. I stayed at the Bachelor Officer Quarter (BOQ) with approximately three hundred foreign officers from many different U.S. allies.

Each week all the officers took field trips to a number of tourist attractions, such as The Smithsonian Institution's National Museum of Natural History, The Empire State Building, Anheuser-Busch Brewery, The Kennedy Space Center, The French Quarter in New Orleans, etc.

While staying in America, I learned about the American Dream – what it meant and its contributions to many people around the world. The "American Dream" was first publicly defined in 1931 by James Truslow Adams in *Epic of America*, as "The American Dream is that dream of a land in which life should be better and richer and fuller for everyone, with opportunity for each according to ability or achievement."

From this definition of the American Dream, I was encouraged and enforced to achieve my dream of becoming a renowned diplomat by working hard. I thought it was the American Dream that contributed to making America rich, strong, and generous. For example, America is rich and generous, because the U.S. Army paid for all of my travel, study, and living in the "fancy BOQ," because the Republic of Korea is a strong ally of the United States.

During the weekends, I was trying to make fact-finding trips to many places to find out to learn about America; why Americans have a higher standard of living; and why many immigrants want to come to the United States, and so on. I also saw many immigrants who came from South America, Asia, Africa, and Europe, enjoying their affordable lifestyle by owning a car and a home, but by working hard.

I studied hard at the U.S. Army Signal School to learn about U.S. Army Signal Corps communication systems and equipment. In addition, I had an opportunity to learn about computers and programming in FORTRAN language. Later, this opportunity led me to specialize in computer science.

While in America, I also enjoyed sightseeing by traveling to thirty states by car and train. By seeing different parts of America and meeting with different types of Americans, I learned more about the American Dream that contributed to what America is today.

I concluded America is the Land of Opportunity for Americans and immigrants, where if they work hard, they could be successful, unlike many other countries where no matter how hard they work they suffer from poverty and economic hardship.

In summary, God led me to achieve this milestone set in accordance with God's plan for me (Proverbs 16:9).

5.9 Milestone 6: God Led Me to Marry Mokjah Kim to Adopt Us as His Son and Daughter

I returned to Korea in May 1966 after I studied and traveled in America for one year. As I expected, I was assigned to teach at the ROK Army Signal School in Daejeon, Korea. I worked hard to transfer the knowledge and skills I acquired from the U.S. Army Signal School to ROK Army soldiers. I also tutored a high school boy who was a son of the Police Department Chief, Chung Nam. The boy's father told me that he hired several tutors for his son, but all failed and left within a week because his son was so rough, defiant, and rebellious.

I took the job because the boy's father offered me a high tutoring compensation and he asked me to live in his home, saving me a great deal of room and board. The boy was taller than me and did not listen to me. I came up with a strategy. I told him that I had stayed in America for one year and showed him many pictures taken. He hated all the courses except English. I started teaching him speaking and listening in English. He started having an interest in English course. Before long, he scored the highest score in English. His teacher and father were happy about his progress.

I was also busy dating a girl who worked at the City Hall. However, I did not have much time to date because I was so busy teaching soldiers at the ROK Army Signal School and tutoring the "rough" boy at home.

Less than a year after I started teaching at the ROK Army Signal School, I took a routine physical examination that included an X-ray test. The Army physician asked me to take another X-ray test for my lungs. I was shocked at the result of the second

X-ray test. The doctor told me that he found a small soft spot inside my lung, which suggested tuberculosis (TB). Although I felt healthy, I was scared at the doctor's announcement that TB usually affects the lungs, but it can also affect other parts of my body, such as the brain, kidneys, or spine.

The doctor asked me to choose whether I would be hospitalized to cure TB or continue to work, taking the medicine regularly and diligently. I had no choice but to take the latter because any record of hospitalization would ruin my military career.

I started taking the medicine faithfully. May times, I had to buy the medicine at drug stores. Luckily I found a pharmacy called Han II Pharmacy in front of the house where I tutored the high school boy. I showed the prescription to the pharmacist who always gave me encouragement.

The pharmacist's name was Mokjah Kim. I felt scared and struggled between being hospitalized and continuing to work at the ROK Army Signal School. However, Miss Kim tried to comfort me by saying, "Lieutenant Sohn, many Koreans are infected by TB, but they do not realize they have TB, because they don't take X-ray tests like you unless they become seriously ill." She further convinced me that I would be cured if I took the medicine regularly, which is also what the Army doctor told me. Because of Miss Kim's kindness and comfort, I went to her pharmacy often, not only to buy the medicine but also bandages and soft drinks.

Although my symptom was not worse, it did not get better either. Despite Miss Kim's continuing encouragement, I had to think about my health before I worried about my military career. After a few weeks of serious consideration, I finally decided to be hospitalized to cure TB at the Army hospital in Miryang far away from Daejeon, about three hours by train.

I stayed at the Army hospital for about six months taking the medicine regularly, exercising regularly, reading books, and writing letters to Miss Kim. Miss Kim started calling me *opba*, a nickname for an elder brother; she was the eldest daughter with five younger brothers and sisters. I accepted being her *opba* happily because I had no sisters. Miss Kim and I became more than friends; we were like brother and sister.

I took another X-ray test, which showed a substantial improvement with the soft spot hardened. However, the doctor recommended I continue to take the medicine regularly. I returned to the ROK Army Signal School, but I was not assigned to a teaching post mainly because of the record that I was hospitalized.

As a result, I decided to be discharged for a medical reason. I applied for a medical discharge from the Army, which was accepted effective December 31, 1967. My military life ended as of December 31, 1967, after ten years of military service-- four years at KMA and six years for active service.

On May 15, 1968, I proposed to Mokjah to marry me and she accepted my proposal. On June 15, 1968, Mokjah and I had a wedding ceremony in Seoul with our families, relatives, and friends celebrating our marriage.

In hindsight, God led me to suffer from the tuberculosis and find Mokjah Kim so I had no choice but to marry her in 1968. She changed my life. Most importantly, it was she who converted me to Christianity and helped me fulfill the milestones I set. Without

Mokjah's hard work and sacrifice while living in America, I could not have completed my Master's degree. I had no scholarships for my tuition. I had a student loan from a local bank for my tuition and living expenses to support us and our son, Gene. My wife worked at a pharmaceutical company in New Jersey on a rotating shift. Sometimes, she worked at night and I had to babysit our boy. My wife changed her legal name to "Kim Sohn" from "Mokjah Kim" when she became a U.S. citizen.

In 1981, I had to go to Saudi Arabia to work for a computer company owned by one of the Saudi princes. Mokjah had to take care of educating the two boys, Gene and Eddie, including their extracurricular activities, such as playing piano and soccer. She also worked at a local department store to support our living expenses.

In 1998, she cofounded Global Children Foundation, Inc. (GCF), a charity organization, which has helped support underprivileged children throughout the world. She was instrumental in setting up GCF as a 501(c)(3) nonprofit organization, a membership database, and branch chapters in major cities U.S., Korea, Japan, and China. She had worked as the Executive Director, President, and Chairperson for GCF until December 31, 2015.

More importantly, Mokjah has been not only my lifetime companion but also a prayer partner for all my life. She prayed hard for me and my work. I would not be what I am without her continuing prayers (1 Thessalonians 5:17).

In summary, God led me to achieve this milestone set in accordance with God's plan for me (Proverbs 16:9).

5.10 Milestone 7: God Led Me to Dream of My American Dream

I lived in Seoul. Staying at home, I started looking for a job in Seoul. I saw an employment advertisement that a news agency in Seoul needed reporters. I was hired as one of the four reporters after passing a set of tough written examinations and interview process. My primary job as a reporter was to translate the news reports issued by the Associated Press (AP) into Korean for all the Korean language newspapers. I was also responsible for reporting many corrupt and unjust articles.

Sometimes, I hated to dig out and write those articles as a reporter. I was also reminded the society in Korea was much different from the United States of America where I stayed for one year. This is why I decided to go to America to study. I wanted to receive a doctoral degree and become a world-renowned professor so I could contribute to changing the Korean society. Then, I took TOEFL test and scored very high. I received an acceptance letter to study at Monmouth College, located near the U.S. Army Signal School.

Despite my unhappiness as a reporter, I could not but brag about my first civilian job and admission to Monmouth College to Miss Kim by letters and phone calls. I asked her to visit me in Seoul. We started dating in Seoul and Incheon. I started falling in love with her. I wrote many letters and mailed popular women's magazines to her.

In May 1968, I finally decided to propose to her, not only because I loved her, but because I felt she could be the only companion who could comfort me forever, knowing my health problem. First, I wrote appealing letters to Miss Kim's father to approve our marriage. Finally, they approved our marriage.

We were married on June 15, 1968, at one of the wedding halls in Seoul with all of our relatives and friends attending. My wife sold her pharmacy in Daejeon and bought another pharmacy in Seoul called Jeki Pharmacy. We started enjoying our happy married life at our home in Seoul.

I planned to work for the news agency until June 30, 1968 to apply for an F-1 visa to go to America on August 1, 1968. The U.S. Embassy required any visa applicants accompany a health report certified by Severance Hospital. So I applied for a health report to Severance Hospital with a set of the X-ray films released by the Army that certified my TB was cured. Unfortunately, however, the doctors at Severance Hospital ruled my TB was not cured, but active. So I could not get the visa, nor would I be able to go to America on August 1, 1968.

This was one of the corruptive realities spread over the country. Then I went to different hospitals to check whether my TB was cured or not. They all proved my TB was cured completely. I visited the Chair of the X-ray Department and showed all the evidence collected. He continued to deny a health certificate for me to apply for a visa to go to America. At this time, I was upset, and I showed my ID as a new reporter to the Chair of X-Ray Department. As soon as he saw my ID, he issued a health certificate that my TB was completely cured and healed. Finally, I received an F-1 visa from the U.S. Embassy. Obviously, he did what he did because he was afraid I would report to the society what he and his department personnel did for my case. This incident was one proof that the Korean society in the 1960s was corrupt, unfair, and unjust, indirectly helping me to determine to achieve my lifetime vision "to transform the Korean society and ultimately the entire world." My wife and I decided to go to America to study and become a famous professor as our first step. In other words, she helped me dream of the American Dream. In summary, God led me to achieve this milestone preset in accordance with God's plan for me (Proverbs 16:9).

CHAPTER 6

MILESTONE 8: GOD LED ME TO ACQUIRE LEADERSHIP AND MANAGEMENT EXPERIENCE

6.1 Arrival in America as an F-1 Student

On October 1, 1968, I arrived at Asbury Park, near Fort Monmouth, New Jersey, where I studied at the U.S. Army Signal School in 1966. I was enrolled at Monmouth College for two semesters.

I invited my wife, Mokjah, to join me as a wife of an F-1 student. However, the Korean government did not allow a spouse of any international student to go abroad under a policy to save the foreign currency of Korea.

I made many American friends when I was at the U.S. Army Signal School at Fort Monmouth. Those friends kept me asking when they could see Mokjah. When I explained the reason why she could not come to join me, they wanted to help me. They wrote a petition to their congressman, requesting him to help Mokjah join me. The Congressman wrote a letter to the U.S. Secretary of State, who in turn requested the Foreign Minister of the Republic of Korea to allow Mokjah to join me.

She finally came to JFK on July 11, 1969. We lived in an attic-room apartment in Asbury Park, New Jersey. I also bought a small used car. One year later, our oldest son was born on April 22, 1970 (Earth Day). We named him Gene, who graduated from MIT with a bachelor's degree in Computer Science and Engineering. Our second son, Edward born in 1973 received a bachelor's degree in English from the University of Maryland.

In 1970, I was admitted to the Master of Science in Electrical Engineering Program at Rutgers University. I majored in Computer Engineering with a concentration in Computer Science. I graduated with an MSEE from Rutgers in 1972. My wife came to America from Korea to join me in Asbury Park, N.J. in 1968. Then, my wife and I received green cards from the United States of America through my wife's pharmacy license.

6.2 Master's Degree in EE with Computer Science Concentration

I received a Master's Degree in Electrical Engineering with Computer Science Concentration from Rutgers in 1972. Although my major was in Electrical Engineering, I took more courses in Computer Science. I took some FORTRAN programming courses while I was stationed at the U.S. Army Signal School in 1956. This programming experience helped not only my study for my Master's degree program, but also finding jobs after graduation.

6.3 Lawful Permanent Resident and U.S. Citizenship

In the 1970s, Lawful Permanent Resident (LPR) was issued to most Master's degree holders or those who had professional licenses. My wife was a pharmacist in Korea. So we both applied for LPRs. Within six months, we received them in 1973.

In 1977, my wife and I received naturalized citizenships from the United States of America. Two boys, Gene, and Edward were born in 1970 and 1973, respectively.

6.4 Attractive Job Offers from Computer Systems Companies

I worked as a communication officer for the Korean Amy, which used U.S. Signal Corps communication equipment, for five years before I came to America. Many of the companies where I applied for a job recognized my experience with the military communication equipment comparable to the U.S experience.

In addition to my academic and practical experience, I was a U.S. citizen. For this reason, a number of companies in New Jersey offered me an attractive job in terms of salary and job functions. On the other hand, many doctoral degree holders were not able to find jobs easily due to the oil crisis, which began in October 1973. So I felt fortunate and thanked God for blessing me.

I finally accepted a job as an electronic engineer at Litton Industries, Inc., which was one of the large IT companies. I was an engineer assigned to work on the Point of Sale (POS) systems for one year. Later, I was transferred to Monroe Calculator Division of Litton Industries, Inc. to work as an electronic systems engineer. Although I had a Master's degree, I lacked a practical experience in designing calculators based on Transistor-to-Transistor Logic (TTL). This was the reason I was not assigned to the design team, but the testing team.

6.5 Microprocessor-based System Design Professional

In November 1971, Intel Corporation invented and publicly introduced the Intel 4004, which was the world's first single chip microprocessor. The 4004 was a four-bit CPU with over 2,000 transistors, and it ran at a clock speed of over 700 kHz. This invention of computer-on-the chip was the advent of the personal computer revolution.

Monroe Calculator Company tried to design, manufacture, and sell more competitive calculators with respect to the size, speed, and price. In 1972, Intel Corporation offered a few calculator companies to design their calculators based on Intel 4004 chip, because the 4004 was best suited for the calculator markets.

In 1972, I was selected to take an extensive training to learn everything about how to apply the 4004 to designing calculators at Intel Corporation in Palo Alto, California. My training lasted for six months. While at Intel Corporation, I worked hard to master the application of the 4004 processor in all aspects, including hardware design and assembly language programming.

After I had returned to Monroe, I recommended the TTL-based calculators be replaced by 4004-based calculators to reduce physical sizes and run faster. However, I was assigned to develop a prototype calculator based on the 4004. I used the same existing flow charts to develop calculator-function algorithms.

After I had returned to Monroe, I helped our team develop a prototype based on a 4004 microprocessor chip. The prototype was successful. Later, the team succeeded in converting the

TTL-based calculators to 4004-based calculators, reducing not only physical sizes but also prices.

Later, Intel Corporation invented 4040, 8008, and 8080 microprocessors, which were much more powerful than 4004, the first-generation microprocessor. The 8008 and 8080 were used to replace a large number of TTL-based or mechanical systems, such as calculators, point-of-sale (POS) systems, automotive functions, and word processors.

In 1974, I was scouted to work for Addressograph-Multigraph Corp. to design word processing systems based on 8080. I was the software manager to design and develop AMTXT word processing systems.

6.6 Minicomputer-based System Design Professional

In 1978, I worked for Lockheed Corporation in Plainfield, New Jersey to work as a senior systems engineer to design the operating system for air traffic flight patterns based on minicomputers.

In 1979, I was offered a position as a senior research engineer to work for the Korea Army Telecommunications Research Laboratory in Seoul. However, I had two boys born in America, and they did not want to move to Korea. As a result, I did not accept the offer. Instead, I moved to Washington, D.C. with a long-term plan to create my own business in information technology systems.

6.7 International Computers & Telecommunications, Inc. (ICT)

In 1981, I founded a company based on my extensive background in computers and telecommunications, using $1,000 working capital in Rockville, Maryland.

I had the first contract to work for an information technology company owned by a Saudi princess. I worked in Riyadh, Saudi Arabia for seven months. I developed a financial management system based on many different HP computers.

In 1982, ICT received the $4.5 million contract from the U.S. Housing and Urban Development (HUD) Agency to maintain its worldwide financial systems. Later, ICT was awarded a $15 million contract to design, develop, and install Low-Level Wind Shear Alert Systems (LLWAS) at 110 major civilian airports in the U.S.

ICT received a number of other federal government contracts from defense and civilian agencies. One of the largest defense contracts was the Theater Automated Command and Control Information Systems for the U.S. Forces in Korea. In order to design, develop, operate, and maintain TACCIMS cost-effectively, I founded a subsidiary company in Korea called Global Tech Co. LTD.

International Computers & Telecom, Inc. (ICT)

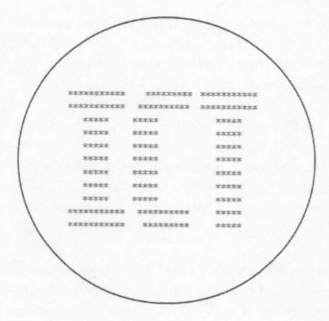

Founder and CEO: David Sohn

Founded in: 1981

6.8 Leadership and Management Education at Harvard Business School (HBS)

Although I was confident in all aspects of technical areas, I did not have formal education in managing personnel, projects, and contracts.

Among a number of management programs, HBS offered me a program called Owner/President Management (OPM) Program. Interestingly, HBS OPM had nicknames such as, "Other People's Money" and, "Office of Personnel Management." The OPM Program had a unique qualification for enrollment. The applicant for the program must be an owner and president of a company whose annual revenue is, at least, $10 million, and the applicant should be able to attend short sessions living in a dormitory each year for three years.

I was one of 110 students who enrolled in OPM 17 in 1991. The students were virtually from all over the world, including North America, Europe, Asia, Africa, Australia, and South America. Most students were from America, Australia, England, Puerto Rico, and Germany.

Marketing strategies and human resources management (HRM) were most beneficial and applicable to my own company, ICT, among many subject areas.

One of the marketing theories known as SWOT (strengths, weaknesses, opportunities, and threats) Analysis contributed to ICT winning a large number of federal, and international contracts, including Incheon International Airport (IIA) construction contract awarded from the Korean government.

After graduation, each of us was awarded a certificate and became an alumnus of Harvard University. There were a large number of executive education programs at HBS, but I heard OPM is the most profitable program, because all the students were owners/presidents of successful corporations. Each HBS program runs an alumni reunion. OPM 17's first reunion was held in Washington, D.C. My wife and I invited our classmates to our home in Potomac, Maryland. We hosted a reception for all the attendees.

In the following year, the classmates in Australia hosted the second OPM 17 reunion. The third-year reunion was held in Puerto Rico. The fourth reunion was held in Germany.

Dad, are you studying?

HARVARD UNIVERSITY
GRADUATE SCHOOL OF BUSINESS
ADMINISTRATION

DAVID YOUNGWHAN SOHN

HAS SUCCESSFULLY COMPLETED
THE 17TH SESSION OF THE
OWNER/PRESIDENT
MANAGEMENT PROGRAM

IN WITNESS WHEREOF THE
OFFICIAL SIGNATURES AND SEAL
ARE HERETO AFFIXED

DONE AT BOSTON, MASSACHUSETTS,
THIS TWENTY-FOURTH DAY OF MAY, NINETEEN NINETEEN AND NINETY-ONE

CHAIRMAN, OWNER/PRESIDENT MANAGEMENT PROGRAM

DEAN OF THE FACULTY

Harvard graduate

6.9 Incheon International Airport (IIA), Korea

In 1991, the Korean government issued a request for a proposal to develop and install Incheon International Airport (IIA), after Bechtel Corporation completed a master plan for IIA.

Airports are divided into three major functional areas: runways for planes to take off and land, terminal buildings to hold passengers before they board and after they arrive, and technical systems such as radars, air traffic controls, computers, and communications.

ICT did not have a corporate experience in constructing international airports. However, ICT was the prime contractor to develop and install Lowe-Level Wind Shear Alert Systems (LLWAS) for 110 U.S. civilian airports. When I tried to introduce the LLWAS to the Korean government in 1991, I found out that the Korean government issued a Request for Proposal (RFP) to develop and construct Incheon International Airport (IIA) as a turnkey system.

By reviewing the RFP, I found out that Bechtel Corporation had completed the Master Plan for IIA, which recommended IIA be constructed on an artificially created manmade land between Yeongjong and Yongyu Islands. I also found Bechtel Corporation would form a consortium with Hyundai Construction to respond to the RFP.

In response to the RFP, I formed ICT Consortium consisting of four companies: ICT, Parsons Company, Turner Construction Company, and Korea Electric Power Corporation (KEPCO). I was a consortium leader of the four companies. ICT was responsible for all technical fields, such as radar, safety and security systems, computers, and communication equipment. Parsons was responsible for constructing the terminal buildings. Turner was responsible for constructing runways. KEPCO was a liaison between the ICT Consortium and the Korean government.

It was reported that Fluor Daniel, Inc. teamed with POSCO as a consortium. Both Bechtel and Fluor Daniel Consortiums were considered the strong competitors, not only because they had extensive experiences in constructing international airports throughout the world, but also because Bechtel completed the two-year IIA Master Plan.

I used SWOT Analysis and Sun Tzu's theory, *The Art of War* as the key winning strategies to respond to the RFP. Tzu's theory states, "If you know your enemy and yourself, you can win a hundred battles (知彼知己 百戰百勝)."

I started extensive detailed analyzes of the background of ICT Consortium and its other competitors because both SWOT and Sun Tzu theories are based on strengths and weaknesses of "myself and my enemy."

As a result of these analyzes, ICT hired two major subcontractors to supplement the weaknesses. ICT Consortium won the Contract because it scored higher marks in the following areas:

Technical merits:

ICT Consortium used a company, namely ICT.

Bechtel Consortium used individual consultants to save overhead cost.

FAA Contract Experience:

ICT had an FAA Contract: to develop and install Low-Level Wind Shear Alert Systems (LLWAS) at 110 U.S. airports.

FAA Regulations:

ICT hired a number of retired FAA directors and employees who were familiar with the FAA regulations.

After ICT Consortium turned the entire construction program to IIA management team, Incheon International Airport was awarded the best airport worldwide by **Airports Council International** (**ACI**) from 2006 to 2011.

ICT's successful completion of the IIA construction helped ICT win more airport-related contracts from other airports, including Cheju International Airport, Chiang Kai-Shek International Airport, and Sung Shan Airport.

Analysis & Comparison

Criteria	Turnkey Airport System Experience	Co. Size (Revenue & Employees)	Overhead Expense	FAA Compliance		Responsibilities for Technical Systems (Co. vs. Individuals)
				FAA Contract Experience	Former FAA Employees	
Enemy	S	S	W	W	W	W
Myself	W	W	S	S	S	S

Analysis & Comparison
(With Subcontractors)

Criteria	Turnkey Airport System Experience	Co. Size (Revenue & Employees)	Overhead Expense	FAA Compliance		Responsibilities of Technical Systems (Co. vs. Individuals)
				FAA Contract Experience	Former FAA Employees	
Enemy	S	S	W	W	W	W
Myself	W	W	S	S	S	S

6.10 Theater Army Command Control Information System (TACCIMS)

ICT was awarded one of the large U.S. Forces Korea contracts, called Theater Army Command Control Information System (TACCICS) in 1993. ICT developed, operated, and maintained TACCIMS contract based in Korea for more than ten years. In order to support this contract cost-effectively, ICT founded a subsidiary called Global Tech, Co., Limited in Seoul, Korea. Global Tech provided technical and logistics support for TACCICS contract and Incheon International Airport contract and Jeju International Airport contract.

6.11 Domestic and International Branches and Subsidiaries

As ICT grew internationally, it opened and operated a large number of branches and subsidiaries not only in the major cities of the United States, but also in foreign countries, as listed below.

U.S. Cities:

- Gaithersburg, MD

- Lanham, MD

- Crystal City, VA

- New York, NY

- Chicago, IL

- Atlanta, GA

- Los Angeles, CA

- Point Mugu Naval Air Station, Camarillo, CA

- San Diego, CA

- Seattle, WA

- Honolulu, HI

Foreign Countries:

- Seoul, Korea: ICT Branch and Subsidiary (Global Tech, Co. Ltd.)

- Kowloon, Hong Kong: ICT Subsidiary (Global Aviation Systems, Inc.)

- Okinawa, Japan: ICT Branch

- Taipei, Taiwan: ICT Branch

- Perth, Australia: ICT Branch

- Manheim, Germany: ICT Branch

- Dar es Salaam, Tanzania

- Nairobi, Kenya

6.12 Fastest-Growing Private Company

ICT grew rapidly and successfully. In 1991 through 1993, ICT was awarded as the Fastest-Growing Private Company in the East Coast by *The Fast 50s*. In 1993, the Inc 500 ranked ICT as the 76th Fastest-Growing Private Company in America, as shown below.

ICT was presented an Equal Opportunity Employer Award from the Mayor and Council, Human Rights Commission and Rockville Chamber of Commerce in 1989. David Sohn received Businessman of the Year Award from William Donald Schaefer, Governor of Maryland in 1993.

THE INC. 500: AMERICA'S FASTEST-GROWING PRIVATE COMPANIES

Inc.

INTERNATIONAL
COMPUTERS &
TELECOMMUNICATIONS

#76

The

500

OCT. 1992/$3.00

6.13 Awards and Recognitions from Public and Private Organizations

David Sohn was invited to visit the United States Presidents at the White House and other places in recognition of ICT's successful international growth in information technology and airport construction businesses.

My wife and I met a number of federal- and state-level politicians, including Maryland Governor Glenn Denning, Congressman Connie Morella, U.S. Senator Elizabeth Dole, and Senators Paul Sarbanes and Chuck Robb.

In 2014, I was invited to a picnic called "Senator Warner's (almost) Annual Pig Roast Games" held at his farm in King George, Virginia.

Elected officials at the State and County governments who have inspired and advised me in many areas include Chap Petersen, Virginia State Senator, David Bulova, Virginia State Delegate, and Sharon Bulova, Chairman of the Fairfax County Board of Supervisors.

To David Sohn,
with best wishes,
G. Bush

To David and Gene, Best Wishes,

6.14 Holes-in-One in 2000 and 2012

I found out that golfing is similar to running a business. Before I hit any ball, I have to plan not only for managing the entire eighteen holes but also for each and every hole. Even I if I missed the drive shot, I strived to recover from the failure on the first hole on the second shot, third shot, and so on, until I succeeded. I used the same strategy for managing businesses. This was the reason why I loved golfing and was called a "golf nut."

Hitting a hole-in-one is every golfer's dream. However, they know it is not easy, no matter how well they play. Even professional golfers seldom hit hole-in-one shots. However, I had a glory of hitting two hole-in-one shots. On August 20, 2000, I hit a hole-in-one shot on the seventeenth hole of 182 yards of Indian Spring Country Club in Silver Spring, Maryland, while playing in a foursome. The other one was hit at the par-three hole of 165 yards of MicroWest Golf Club in Orlando, Florida while playing with three other golfers.

I have been living in the Tournament Players Club (TPC) in Avenel Farm in Potomac, Maryland. In 2013, I was playing golf at TPC on Sunday. Then I noticed Vice President Joe Biden playing golf, following my team. A number of security personnel followed our team closely. As soon as I finished the eighteenth hole, I watched the Vice President putt on the eighteenth hole outside of the green. After finishing his putting, he kindly volunteered to pose a picture with my teammate and me.

6.15 Publishing The Korean American Life Magazine

I wanted to inspire Korean Americans to participate in mainstream America in different aspects of their American life, rather than cling to their own cultures. I wanted them to compete with the mainstream Americans in business, politics, education, sports, journalism, and community services, rather than compete against Korean Americans. This was the reason I published the *Korean American Life* (*KAL*) magazine in Korean and English in color on a monthly basis.

I spent, at least, $50,000 to publish the *KAL* magazine monthly and distribute them to the Korean Americans throughout the United States, using the ICT branch offices. I also traveled nationwide to discover the most successful Korean Americans in mainstream America. In cooperation with *KAL* magazine, I sponsored the Mainstream American Award Banquet annually during which I recognized the Korean Americans who were most successful in participating in mainstream America.

The First Annual
MAINSTREAM AMERICA AWARDS
for
EXCELLENCE

제1회 최우수 한인교포 표창 및 시상식

April 19, 1991
6:00 p.m. ~ 11:00 p.m.

Tysons Corner Marriott Hotel
Vienna, Virginia

The Korean-American Life Magazine

6.16 Our Christian Faith and Prayers

My wife Kim had become a Christian before she came to America in 1969. She tried to convert me to Christianity. However, with my strong background in science and technology acquired through formal education and extensive experience, it was not easy for me to believe in the Bible, including the birth and resurrection of Jesus Christ and parting of the Red Sea.

When I was in Saudi Arabia, I began to realize there have been many miracles in the history of mankind, and there must be a supernatural being that causes miracles that are unscientific to occur. I believed the supernatural being is God. Once I conceived and accepted this concept, I believed in everything in the Bible and decided to accept Jesus Christ as my personal Lord and Savior and became baptized.

Kim and I have attended Global Mission Church (GMC) in Silver Spring, Maryland every week, since 1980s. We attend church worship services on Sundays. We also watch Rev. Joel Osteen's televised sermons every Sunday before we go to our main church. We enjoy listening to Joel's preaching that always starts with "something funny." We also love to read and meditate Joel's daily email sent with "today's scripture, preaching, and a prayer for today."

We also listen to Sunday morning radio broadcast called "So What?" of Senior Pastor Lon Solomon of McLean Bible Church, Tysons, VA, on our way to Global Mission Church. If we arrive at church too early, we stay in the car until Pastor Solomon completes his sermon. We also visit McLean Bible Church to attend worship service.

Kim and I believe in the power of our prayers. Kim who belongs to GMC's Prayer Group dedicates several hours per week to prayers for our family, relatives, friends, the country, and the entire world.

Thus, we obey God's commandment, "Pray without ceasing." (1 Thessalonians 5:17, NIV)

6.17 OmniBio Secure, Inc.

In 2000, I founded a research and development (R&D) company called OmniBio Secure, Inc., based on multiple biometric technologies using fingerprint and iris software algorithms. I was fascinated by the software technology to identify individuals. Although the fingerprint technology had been used for a longer period, there were inherent problems with identification algorithms, because fingerprints are worn out, grown, or messed up by dirty materials. Iris algorithms are reliable, but again they cannot be perfect. There is no a single biometrical technology that produces a perfect identification. However, two or more technologies can produce one hundred percent accuracy in identifying individuals.

For this reason, I used two technologies: fingerprint and iris recognitions. Because the biometrical technologies needed a large number of pattern-recognition software algorithms, I needed to use a large number of software design and test engineers.

Instead of hiring many software personnel, I decided to buy a biometric software development company through nationwide M&A companies to save development time.

6.18 Sale of ICT

While hunting a software development company, an M&A company introduced a number of companies to buy ICT which was a successful international company engaged in IT and airport construction with a large number of domestic and foreign branches and subsidiaries.

It was not easy for me to run two companies concurrently in terms of manpower and overhead expenses. Therefore, I finally decided to sell ICT and focus on OmniBio Secure, Inc. in 2000.

6.19 Importance of Security since September 11, 2001 Terrorist Attack

After the 9/11 terrorist attack had occurred, the value of OmniBio Secure, Inc. soared all of a sudden, because the biometrical technology is the best method for detecting and identifying terrorist suspects.

6.20 Retirement from Business

After I sold ICT, I tried to focus on expanding operations of OmniBio Secure, Inc. for security applications. However, I decided to dissolve the company and retire from the business in 2002.

In summary, God led me to achieve this milestone set in accordance with God's plan for me (Proverbs 16:9).

CHAPTER 7

MILESTONE 9: GOD LED ME TO FULFILL MY AMERICAN DREAM

7.1 God's "Purposeful Detour"

In 1968, I came to America as a student. Since then, God led me to receive a Master's degree successfully, found and run International Computers & Telecom, Inc. (ICT) successfully, and acquire extensive corporate experiences in leadership and management.

As a result of ICT's successful growth as an international company engaged in IT and airport construction, ICT and I received a wide variety of awards and recognitions from the public and private sectors. With these valuable awards and recognitions, I enjoyed participating in Mainstream America, meeting with high-level public and private celebrities.

God blessed my family and me so we could afford to live in a house in a two-acre lot. The house had nine bedrooms with a full bathroom in each and five fireplaces. We opened our home for church choir practices and invited a large number of business-related personnel, especially employees, consultants, and contract personnel from Global Tech, Co. Ltd., Korea.

I used to drive American-made automobiles, but I realized personal safety is important. One day, the sales person of a Mercedes-Benz loaned a brand new model of Benz 600, which was the top of all the models to me to test-drive for one month free of charge. I drove a big Cadillac at that time. The salesperson made a joke about the safety. If you drive a Benz 600 and hit a Cadillac, you will be safe.

After I had driven Benz 600, I found it smooth and safe. So I bought the car. Thanking God for His blessing of my family and business, I changed the license plate of my car to "PHIL413." Sometimes, people commented, "I like that verse very much too." Other people greeted me as a fellow Christian.

In 2002, I retired from that business after I had a successful business. First and foremost, I thanked God for blessing my family and leading me to manage ICT successfully. I said to myself, "Dear God, I thank you for making it possible for me to achieve the American Dream I dreamed of in 1968 when I came to America."

As soon as I prayed, I realized I failed to fulfill my original American Dream, which was to "obtain a doctoral degree in America and become a world-renowned professor." Although I was financially successful and I was recognized by the Mainstream America as a successful businessman, I did not receive a doctoral degree and did not become a professor.

This was the momentum and turning point – to decide to fulfill my American Dream. God intentionally detoured me to take a different route before I fulfilled my American Dream, so I could not only be financially successful but also acquire extensive experiences in leadership and management. God thought I needed such financial affordability and leadership and management experiences for me to achieve God's plan for me successfully.

7.2 Doctor of Management in Organizational Leadership

I deferred my doctoral program not only because I was not able to become a full-time student, but also because I was more successful with a Master's degree than doctoral degree holders.

In any event, I looked for a university where I could complete a doctoral degree as a full-time student. I thought about Harvard Business School where I studied for several months in three different years or Rutgers University where I received a Master's degree.

However, I was concerned about the possibility it would take me a few years to complete a doctoral degree living far away from home. It was also difficult for me to decide what program to major in. I completed all the doctoral coursework in the Computer Science program. However, I founded and managed IT companies for more than twenty-five years. Therefore, I wanted to major in a program other than IT. Therefore, I wanted to focus on leadership and management.

While I was hesitant, a University of Phoenix recruiter called me and offered me a Doctor of Management in Organizational Leadership program. When I complained about living in Phoenix for three years or more, he explained to me about the doctoral program in detail. I could complete all the coursework online through distance education. I had a great deal of online communications through ICT. I also designed and sold dial-up corporate network programs in the late 1970s. I had another interest in the online doctoral program; I was interested in inventing a state-of-the-art online education program by using fingerprinted mice and web cameras to ensure online students cannot cheat or commit plagiarism.

The curriculum of Doctor of Management Program attracted me. So in 2004, I was enrolled in the Doctor of Management in Organizational Leadership program. All the coursework was completed online. I had to be in Phoenix to write my dissertation. I was interested in developing a national security system based on biometric technologies. I also had to conduct an extensive survey for my dissertation by using students and employees of two large community colleges in Los Angeles. I used 1,220 samples for my survey.

7.3 Title of My Dissertation

"An Analysis of Voluntary National Biometric Identification Cards as Means to Prevent Identity Fraud."

Abstract

Identify fraud has emerged as a serious problem because of global terrorism. The 9/11 hijackers obtained drivers' licenses fraudulently and used them to board airplanes. To prevent terrorists from using fraudulent identification documents, the Intelligence Reform and Terrorism Prevention Act required the use of biometric identifier technology and personal identification cards. The purpose of this quantitative research study was to examine the motivational factors for the public to use voluntary biometric identification cards (NBICs) as a more reliable and secure means to prevent identity fraud. The survey sample was 1,220 students, faculty, and employees of two community colleges in California. The survey results suggested that the public would use voluntary NBICs if certain incentives were available to NBIC users.

It took me about three years to complete the entire coursework, pass the qualifying exam, and write a dissertation. Because I had a lot of time as a retiree and I could afford my schooling and research, I was told my research was one of the best since the University of Phoenix began producing doctoral program students.

In fact, in 2005, I was awarded the Doctoral Student of the Year. My picture and dissertation were introduced and printed in the Annual Report of Apollo Education Group, Inc., University of Phoenix's parent company.

University of Phoenix

Upon the recommendation of the Faculty,
University of Phoenix does hereby confer upon

David Y. Sohn

The Degree of

Doctor of Management

with all the rights, honors and privileges thereunto appertaining.

In witness whereof, the seal of the University and the signature as authorized
by the Board of Directors, University of Phoenix, are hereunto affixed,
this thirty-first day of March, in the year two thousand five.

Chairman, Board of Directors

President

7.4 Professor of Business and Information Systems

As soon as I received a Doctor of Management in Organizational Leadership in 2005, I was invited to teach business and information technology courses for undergraduate and graduate programs at a number of universities in the United States, including University of Phoenix, Grand Canyon University, and Axia College of the University of Phoenix. In 2006, I had to teach five online courses with a total of 105 students per term. I was also invited to develop and teach an information technology for Management course at Washington Baptist University in Virginia in 2007.

While teaching residential and distance education courses, I found a new passion in residential and distance education. Sometimes, I had online students not only in different cities in the U.S., but also in foreign countries, such as Japan (Okinawa).

I was also invited as a guest speaker to speak to Yanbyun University of Science and Technology in China. In 2007, Handong Global University in Korea offered me to teach graduate business program courses.

At the end of 2007, I finally declared to myself that I have achieved the American Dream I dreamed of in 1968, "to obtain a doctoral degree in America and to become a world-renowned professor."

In summary, God led me to achieve this milestone set in accordance with God's plan for me (Proverbs 16:9).

CHAPTER 8

MILESTONE 10: GOD LED ME TO FULFILL GOD'S PLAN FOR ME

8. 1 God's Plan for Me

God created me so I can glorify Him as one of His sons by transforming the world through innovative and effective education provided to all the human beings around the world, including financially, physically, and/or socially underprivileged people.

Fulfilling my American Dream was one of the most important milestones for me to achieve God's plan for me. However, God detoured me to save some money and acquire leadership and management experiences for rainy days. Then God led me to find a new passion in education and gave me confidence in founding a university that can provide innovative and effective education.

8.2 Foundation of IGlobal University in 2008

In 2007, I was offered to teach graduate courses at Handong Global University in Korea. My wife and I planned to relocate to Korea to live for three to five years. However, I found out that I had a severe indigestion problem, and my physician conducted a number of tests. As a result, I decided not to go to Korea. However, my doctors allowed me to continue teaching in America.

In May 2007, I was offered to develop a course called Information Technology for Management for a Christian university in Virginia. The president of this university who knew my background well asked me to submit a comprehensive proposal that would allow the university to offer a distance education program. I spent a great deal of time and effort for this proposal for six months. In December 2007, I did my best to complete my proposal that included my arrangement for thirty computers to be delivered to the university.

Despite the fact that I spent my own time and money for this proposal, the university rejected my proposal, although the president liked it. This was the time when I told myself, "If I had my own university, I could run it with my own ideas."

8.3 State Registration and Certification

On February 4, 2008, I prayed to God and discussed with my wife. Then I decided to found a university called IGlobal University ("IGU") in Fairfax, Virginia. I named it as such to emphasize that IGlobal University will provide "innovative global education."

First, I had to register the university as IGlobal University LLC at the State Corporation Commission. Then I applied for certification of State Council of Higher Education for Virginia (SCHEV) to confer degrees, certificates, and diplomas.

State Council of
Higher Education for Virginia

8.4 IGU's Founding Philosophy

I wanted to make IGU different from other established traditional colleges and universities that admit many students who are normally smart or able to afford it or both. I envisioned creating a university to transform the world by providing the innovative and effective education to not only to Americans, but also all the people around the world, including those who are underprivileged financially, physically, and/or socially.

IGU's founding philosophy was based on the following principles:

FOUR PILLARS FOR INSTITUTIONAL OPERATIONS

IGU is committed to operating the university based on the following principles:

• Legal operations

• One of the laws for IGU to comply with is that IGU provides equal educational and employment opportunities and not to discriminate illegally on the basis of gender, race, national origin, religion, age, marital status, or disability in its educational programs, activities, or its employment and personnel policies.

• Ethical operations

• Professional operations

• Compassionate operations

VISION STATEMENT

IGlobal University will transform the world by providing the most effective education to people around the world for their intellectual, professional, spiritual, and leadership development and growth whether they are young or old, rich or poor, privileged or underprivileged, local or remote.

MISSION STATEMENT

The mission of IGlobal University is to provide a diverse student body with career-related education based on scholarly, innovative, and practical approaches to meet and exceed emerging global challenges, through the following objectives:

- To develop career-related programs and curricular practical training;

- To provide practical training through internships, externships, field trips, and invited guest speakers in close cooperation with the community resources

- To provide students with ongoing career development services

INSTITUTIONAL GOALS

In order to fulfill its mission, the university established the following strategic goals:

- To achieve the academic excellence in career-related education

- To achieve financial sustainability and strength by efficient and effective resource management

- To manage the global expansion and growth successfully

INSTITUTIONAL OBJECTIVES

In order to achieve its strategic goals, the university established the following objectives with emphasis on "academic quality":

- To develop appropriate career-oriented academic programs

- To achieve high enrollment, retention, and placement rates through satisfactory student learning outcomes, graduate satisfaction, and employee satisfaction

- To establish close cooperative partnerships with all the stakeholders, including employers and community leaders at the local, regional, national, and global levels.

CORE VALUES

The essential drive of IGlobal University is reflected in its variety of educational programs offered to worldwide students.

- **Diversity**: IGlobal University welcomes students from all over the world and fosters equal participation of all its constituents.

- **Lifelong Learning**: IGlobal University stimulates and promotes learning and life-long knowledge retention through continuing education.

- **Affirmative Spirit**: IGlobal University promotes integrity and harmonious work with pride and compassion.

- **Partnership Cooperation**: IGlobal University cooperates with all of its stakeholders, including students, faculty, staff, and community citizens.

- **Effective Instructional Delivery**: IGlobal University's educational programs are designed for students who aspire to succeed in many professional areas of study. IGlobal University's instructional delivery is based on primarily residential settings on the main campus and any future branch campus.

ACADEMIC OBJECTIVES

In fulfilling its mission, IGlobal University is committed to the following educational objectives:

- Graduates will accumulate foundational and critical knowledge to work productively in the community.

- Graduates will effectively integrate administrative and management skills to meet the needs of the diverse business community.

- Graduates will apply educational and practical business concepts and administrative skills in their respective fields of work.

- Graduates will continue to pursue self-directed and life-long learning to be current with advanced business operations.

- Graduates will demonstrate competent communication skills in the managing of human resources at the workplace.

- Graduates will exhibit pertinent general knowledge and professional skills for career advancement, leadership roles, and teamwork in an increasingly versatile economy.

- Graduates will demonstrate competency and understanding of functional work areas and exhibit broad expertise in their specific field of study.

8.5 National Accreditation Through 2019

I wanted IGU to be able to admit students from all over the world. I did not know in order for IGU to admit international students, IGU must be accredited by an accrediting agency. So I contacted Distance Education Training Council (DETC) for accreditation so that IGU can immediately admit online students from different states. However, I found out that DETC accreditation alone would not allow IGU to admit international students.

As a result, I contact the Accrediting Council for Independent Colleges and Schools (ACICS). However, I found that IGU must be operational for at least two years and have least seven graduates per program, and ten currently enrolled students at the time of ACICS' visit for initial accreditation. In 2000, IGU applied for initial accreditation with only one program, MBA, to expedite initial accreditation. In April 2012, IGU was awarded institutional initial accreditation for its MBA program. In 2015, IGU was awarded a renewal of accreditation through December 31, 2019.

8.6 ACCREDITED ACADEMIC PROGRAMS

In 2012, IGU was awarded initial accreditation for its MBA program. Later, IGU added accreditation of Bachelor of Science in Information Technology (BSIT), Bachelor of Business Administration (BBA), and English as a Second Language (ESL) programs.

In 2015, IGU was awarded a renewal of accreditation through December 31, 2019. One of the factors that contributed to such a long-term renewal of accreditation was that all the stakeholders at IGU, namely administrative staff, faculty, and students did their best to comply with all the accreditation criteria. In addition, the knowledge and experience I gained as an ACICS Evaluator helped IGU to plan and prepare well for all the renewal activities.

In 2015, IGU added another accredited program called Master of Science in Information Technology (MSIT).

8.7 SEVP Certification

I found out the Student and Exchange Visitor Program (SEVP) certifies accredited institutions to enroll nonimmigrant students (F-1). IGU obtained the SEVP certification for MBA Program in 2013 and BSIT, BBA, and ESL Programs in 2014.

8.8 Title IV Federal Student Aid Loan Program

IGU applied for the Title IV Federal Student Aid Loan Program. In 2013, the U.S. Department of Education (DoE) approved the Federal Student Loan Program for IGU's MBA program. In 2015, IGU applied for the Federal Student Grant Program for BSIT, BBA, and ESL programs.

8.9 Exchange Visitor (J-1) Program

The U.S. Department of State designated IGU as a sponsor of an Exchange Visitor Program in accordance with the administrative regulations issued under the Mutual Educational and Cultural Exchange Act of 1961, with the following approved categories:

Form DS-2019:   Professor, Research Scholar, Specialist, Student, College/University

Form DS-2019   Allotment for the first year of operation: 340

8.10 Annandale and Tysons Campuses

In addition to the main campus, IGU opened an instructional site in Tysons Corner, Virginia, which has three metro stations, two large shopping malls, and many corporations near the campus.

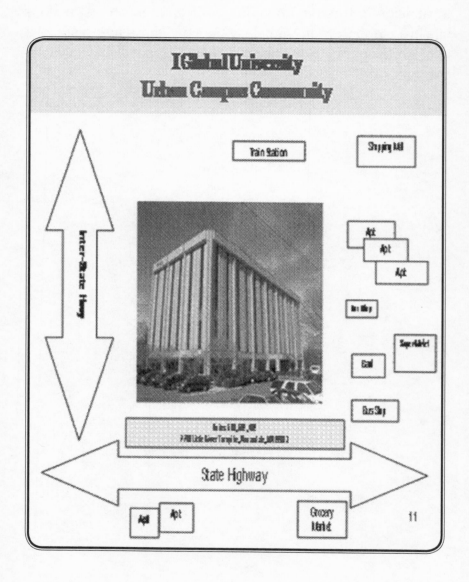

IGlobal University
Urban Campus Community

Train Station

Shopping Mall

Inter-State Hwy

Apt
Apt
Apt

Bus Way

Super Market

School

Bus Stop

State Highway

Apt Apt

Grocery Market

11

Tysons Campus

8133 Leesburg Pike, #260, Vienna, VA 22182

8.11 Diverse Students from Over Thirty Different Countries

IGU enrolls domestic and international students from over thirty different countries mainly in Asia, Africa, and South America.

In summary, God led me to achieve this milestone set in accordance with God's plan for me (Proverbs 16:9).

CHAPTER 9

WITNESSING GOD "TO THE END OF THE EARTH"

IGlobal University ("IGU") is growing successfully because it was one of the milestones set for me by God to achieve His plan for me, "to transform the world through innovative and effective education." IGU will continue to grow to transform the world in the future.

However, God inspired me to disseminate how God blessed my life by publishing my success stories in many different languages. First, God led me to discover His plan for me. Then I realized God does not direct each and every step for me, but leads me to reach the next milestone safely and successfully until the last milestone (Proverbs 16:9).

IGlobal University is a relatively new university through which God helped me to discover and implement His plan for me. Now He wants me to write my success stories in all different languages so that all "Gentiles" can read them and discover God's plan for them.

God wants me to be a witness that God creates each of us with a specific individual plan and directs us to achieve each milestone He set so we can fulfill His plan set for us.

This principle is similar to, or an extension of, His commandments in Mark 28:19 and Acts 1:8, respectively.

"Therefore go and make disciples of all nations, baptizing them in the name of the Father and of the Son and of the Holy Spirit" (Mark 28:19).

"You will receive power when the Holy Spirit has come upon you, and you will be my witnesses in Jerusalem and in all Judea and Samaria, and to the end of the earth" (Acts 1:8).

While IGlobal University is growing successfully, I will continue to disseminate my testimonials in English and other "Gentile" languages until I die so God creates us with a specific individual plan for each of us to prosper and not harm us, and give us hope and a future (Jeremiah 29:11).

I knew God created me in His image (Genesis 1:27) and He knows the plans He has for me. He has plans to prosper me and not to harm me, and plans to give me hope and a future (Jeremiah 29:11). However, I cannot find or identify exactly what His plans for me was and are. In other words, His plans for me are too broad, imaginary, and unspecific.

In 1968, when I was thirty years old, God led me to witness the Korean society that was corruptive, unfair, and unjust, while I worked as a news reporter. I was deeply depressed about the society, country, and the world, as well as about my future. I asked God where were His plans "to prosper me and not harm me" and when He would give me hope and a bright future. I complained to God that I had to resign from my first civilian job as of April 30, 1968.

I tried hard to discover God's plans for me by reviewing and examining thoroughly all the major events I went throughout my thirty years of my life. Finally, I concluded God's plan for me was *to transform the Korean society and later the world through innovative and effective education*. I believed that the corrupt and decayed society in Korea would not change easily or quickly. I believed that it will be possible through appropriate education for generations to come. I would rather try to assume that transforming the world through education was God's plan for me.

Although I discovered God's plan for me, it was too vague and broad. This was when I had a problem of understanding Proverbs 16:9, which says, "A man's heart plans his way, but the Lord directs his steps." I complained if God had a plan for me and directed my steps, why would I go in the wrong direction, as we often do.

At this time, I got a clear answer about Proverbs 16:9. God does not direct each and every step I take, but directs me in the right direction. This was when I conceived of God's milestones set for me to achieve His plan. In other words, He does not direct each and every step for me, but guides me so I can arrive at the next milestone He set for me.

At the same time, I learned God gives me a free will, and He is most pleased when I choose my own steps to arrive at the next milestone, in the same way, God would direct my steps. This is the very reason why He creates us in His image as a creature (Genesis 1:27) but not as His children until we accept Jesus Christ as our personal Lord and Savior (Ephesians 1:5), although He could create us as His children upon our birth.

God could create an eternal life for us when He creates us, but He does not. Rather, He appeals to our own free will. In other words, He wants us to believe in Jesus Christ if we want eternal life (John 3:16). Revelation 3:20 says, "Here I am! I stand at the door and knock. If anyone hears my voice and opens the door, I will come in and eat with that person, and they with me." Jesus could come into our room without knocking on the door and ask us to eat. However, He asks us to open the door if and only if we wish.

More importantly, God does not want us to be His children when He creates us (Genesis 1:27), but when we believe in Jesus Christ (Ephesians 1:5). In other words, He gives us a free will to become His children through Jesus Christ. As a result of this free will, many people die without being His children.

The following is a list of nine milestones I set for me to fulfill God's plan for me:

Milestone 1: God created me in His image (Genesis 1:27).

Milestone 2: God led me to achieve academic superiority.

Milestone 3: God led me to choose Korea Military Academy.

Milestone 4: God led me to study at the U.S. Army Signal School.

Milestone 5: Go led me to witness those who achieved the American Dream.

Milestone 6: God led me to marry Mokjah Kim to adopt us as His Son and Daughter.

Milestone 7: God led me to dream of my American Dream.

Milestone 8: God led me to acquire leadership and management experience.

Milestone 9: God Led Me to Fulfill My American Dream

Milestone 10: God led me to achieve His plan.

The Bible verses, which have helped me discover God's plan and milestones for me and set my own lifetime vision and milestones, include but are not limited to, the following:

1. Genesis 1:27 (NIV)

"So God created mankind in his own image, in the image of God he created them; male and female he created them."

2. Jeremiah 29:11 (NIV)

"'For I know the plans I have for you,' declares the Lord, 'plans to prosper you and not to harm you, plans to give you hope and a future.'"

3. Proverbs 16:9 (NIV)

"In their hearts humans plan their course, but the Lord establishes their steps."

4. Ephesians 1:5 (NIV)

"He predestined us for adoption to sonship through Jesus Christ, in accordance with His pleasure and will."

5. John 3:16 (NIV)

"For God so loved the world that He gave His one and only Son, that whoever believes in Him shall not perish but have eternal life."

6. Revelation 3:20 (NIV)

"Here I am! I stand at the door and knock. If anyone hears My voice and opens the door, I will come in and eat with that person, and they with Me."

7. Mark 28:19 (NIV)

"Therefore go and make disciples of all nations, baptizing them in the name of the Father and of the Son and of the Holy Spirit."

8. Acts 1:8 (NIV)

"You will receive power when the Holy Spirit has come upon you, and you will be my witnesses in Jerusalem and in all Judea and Samaria, and to the end of the earth."

In summary and conclusion, God has blessed me throughout my life since my birth abundantly and richly. Now God wants me to become His witness to disseminate my blessed life. I will continue to spread God's plan and milestones set for each of us to all the Gentiles in different languages, as in His commandments in Mark 28:19 and Acts 1:8.

I want this memoir of mine to be one of the means to inspire both believers and non-believers, especially those who are young, to strive to search for and identify their lifetime vision, as early as possible, based on their faith in and conviction of presumptive God's plan for them. No one is absolutely certain, except God, that their secular vision is exactly identical to God's original plan for him or her – perhaps not until their vision is fulfilled through their faith.

Once their lifetime vision has been set as a result of this process, they must strive to identify and set the milestones for them to fulfill their lifetime vision effectively and successfully. When their milestones are identified and set, they must strive to make their milestones coincide with God's milestones set according to His original plan for them by faith and prayers. In this process, they must be reminded God does not determine each and every step of theirs but directs them in the right direction until they arrive at the next milestone safely and successfully (Proverbs 16:3).

When they execute and achieve their milestones one at a time until the last milestone, their lifetime vision is fulfilled. When their last milestone has been fulfilled, their vision, namely God's plan for them, has been fulfilled, according to His promise in Jeremiah 29:11.